Antoine Predock₃
houses

2

A n t o i n e   P r e d o c k$_3$
houses

edited by Brad Collins

RIZZOLI

For Don Schlegel, and his inspiration

First published in the United States of America in 2000 by
Rizzoli International Publications, Inc.
300 Park Avenue South, New York, New York 10010

Copyright © 2000 Rizzoli International Publications, Inc.

ISBN 0-8478-2259-1 (hardcover)
LC 00-101280

Front cover: Turtle Creek House photographed by Robert Reck,
    courtesy of *Architectural Digest*, © 1994 The Condé Nast
    Publications. All rights reserved. Used with permission.
Front flap: Venice Beach House, photograph © Timothy Hursely
Back cover: Zuber House, photograph © Timothy Hursley
Back flap: Winandy House, photograph by Robert Reck,
    courtesy of *Architectural Digest*, © 1992 The Condé Nast
    Publications. All rights reserved. Used with permission

Design and Composition by
    Group **C** Inc Boston/New Haven (BC, EZ)

Printed and bound in Singapore

CONTENTS

FOREGROUND

Antoine Predock

La Luz [pp. 14-29], a new community on 500 acres outside Albuquerque, was the first complete project that I did on my own. It serves as a foreground to other houses and work, as well as a foreground to my career. It established the principle of honoring the land and set the stage for the site specificity of my work. All of the houses, all of my work, responds to site in particular ways—engaging both the physical and cultural landscape. With La Luz, that response had to do primarily with the notion of community and privacy within an architecture that was an abstracted landform—a surrogate escarpment. My work, the completed houses as well as the four projects presented here, ties together these various trails to make an architecture derived from the circumstances of the client but rooted in the somewhat mysterious realm called "place."

La Luz was also derived from attitudes about site planning with an ecological conscience—a fundamental component that is embodied in various ways in all my work. At La Luz, rather than usurping large areas of the site, the flood plain was protected by organizing the units in tight groupings with common yards and roads.

La Luz was not a "normal" development. It was built in phases, and played out as a laboratory for me: I lived the project through construction, physically working on it, building parts of a play area myself. Phase by phase I learned about nuances of orientation—focused views, response to sun, and many other aspects. Working this way showed me how the seasons act on a building, how time acts on architecture, how we relate to a summer evening in a different way than we do to a fall morning. It was a chance to understand that even though buildings are derived from operations that are somewhat formulaic—wind direction, views, topographic nuances, social and cultural milieu—the architecture has a life of its own, a particular aura. Architecture lives and has many guises beyond the rational—atmospheric, phenomenological, and poetic.

LAKE HOUSE

The site can be thought of as a peninsula defined by creeks on the east and west and a lake to the north. To the west, there is very dense vegetation—a big mulberry tree, a bamboo thicket—and consequently a lot of bird activity. The east end of the site is much more open, with singular, "iconic" trees defining a canopy, and an abrupt slope down to the edge of the water. The house penetrates into the under-story and the bamboo growth and, in an arcing trajectory, ascends to the east.

There is a journey in this house that involves two kinds of ascents. From the centroid of the house—the entry foyer, which also gives access to the master suite—you can either go west, climbing up three stepped, grass terraces to arrive at a trellis: a steel grillage that you can walk across. The steel grillage defines a breezeway below. Continuing from that metal deck, you walk on a glass roof over a bonsai greenhouse to a cypress deck/viewing platform on the west that is for looking out over the lake and watching birds [the owners are avid bird-watchers].

The other journey from the centroid is to the east. It involves going through the public areas of the house—through living, past a screen porch, the kitchen functions—and up a stair to an upper level work-out room/office that is poised in the tree canopy like a tree-house. The arc of the house is an embracing gesture toward the lake that also dodges and accommodates important specimen trees.

The trees create a site matrix with respect to shading, with views to the trees themselves from critical points in the house. This is one of the trails that the house establishes—the tracing of the arcing trajectory. There is also a trail of artifacts—bonsai specimens—in the greenhouse on the west, and also on the terraces. So the terraces are exhibit areas as well as social platforms.

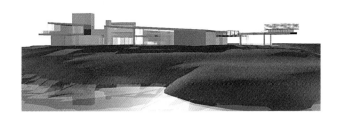

The entry is designed with a quiet pool with a walkway across it. From there, the grass terraces ascend to the west. The grass terraces are framed by two components of the house, the private master suite and the garage/service components which seize and channel the part of the arc that is formed by the terraces. The terraces are isolated and unexpected grass plots, like stair treads, only big ones. They are "grass planes," as opposed to just grass for grass's sake. There is a surreal edge about them. And from the cypress platform, these grass terraces seemingly step down into the earth.

Once you leave the grass terraces, you become weightless. You are walking over air, looking down through grillage, and then down through glass into an intimate greenhouse, seeing bonsai specimens in plan view. The steel armature of the bonsai greenhouse is a structural steel cage that spins off the walkway grillage/grating that lets light through to the breezeway below, and sustains the cantilever of the cypress deck.

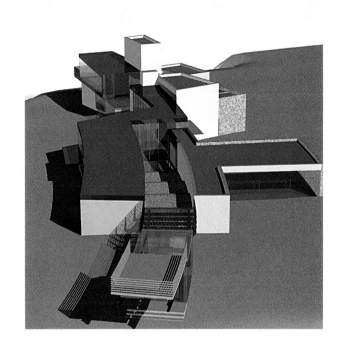

Slicing through all of this is an 8-foot wide water channel that connects the house to the edge of the lake and demonstrates all the states water can have. One section of it is a lap pool. But you don't know that at first glance. You understand it as a continuous zone of water with a different series of intentions about water as it moves from house to lake's edge.

The central body of the house and the garage are clad in stone—the garage is smooth, the rest is rough. These parts of the house are more consolidated and weighty, less ephemeral than the rest. They are about being anchored to earth. Concrete tower elements—circulation tower and fireplace—are inserted into the stone and steel matrix. The roof is copper, wrapping over to become fascias. Notched into the main living space is a screened porch that evokes the atmosphere of "Texas screen porches." There is a fire pit that backs into the fireplace in the living room. As you go west, following the arc, the house gets lighter and lighter. It suggests a Texan snake.

STRATA HOUSE

The site is on the northern flank of Camelback Mountain in Phoenix with a panoramic sweep from northeast to northwest. The house is a diagrammatic series of strata that come out of the earth. There is a matrix of boulders, important rock formations that define the position on the site. The house literally dances around and through these groupings of rocks. One boulder surfaces in the transition zone between living and dining, and another surfaces on a terrace just outside the master suite. One group erupts out of water in the entry court, and another group bookends one end of the pool deck.

As the house adjusts to these formations, weaving through them, the datum strata maintains essentially one plane. It is a topographic bench that the house occupies with a minor level change at the west end to adjust to grade. As the house comes out of the ground, a concrete base parallels the earth-bound qualities of the rock outcroppings. Unlike the Box Canyon house, where the platform is a datum that has a real thickness and absorbs program elements, in this case the strata is more like a plane of rock. At the low end of the site, where the contours fall away, the base is fairly high and assertive, but as it moves from east to west it dissolves into the site.

The drive up the edge of the site pivots around a palo verde tree that nestles up against the kitchen terrace to the east. The garage is tucked behind the house toward the hillside, right on the edge of an arroyo. On arrival, guests park on the apron of the garage and walk under a trellis, through the entry court with the boulder grouping and

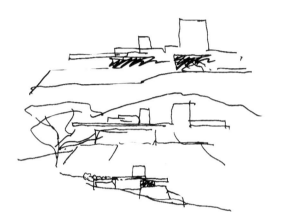

water. This trellis, on the south edge of the entry court, runs perpendicular to a steel canopy that is aimed northward into the main entry. The entry alignment is carved through between the garage and family room, and extends as a bridge to a guest house cut into the hillside across the arroyo. There is a sense of the body of the house being anchored by the promontory-like concrete stratum. This is reaffirmed by the boulders that project through the floor plane.

The same concrete becomes the flooring of the house and is ground, like terrazzo, to reveal the aggregate. The other elements of the base of the house are steel and glass. A study tower emerges from the roof plane to create a high internal volume and provide an elevated observation deck accessed by a stair off of the main roof terrace, which is co-planar with the pool area.

As the house cuts into the hillside, the master bath extends southward. It is a full level below the pool, which has a glazed side that forms a window that illuminates the master bath. It is a water filled aperture of light, with light coming through the pool and through the water. As the water emerges from the hillside in the guise of the pool, it spills over into a garden courtyard adjacent to the master bath. That same line of water is revealed in the master bath itself in the pool aperture.

The fireplace is merged with the boulder in the living room and terminates the view axis from the front door. There is also an external fireplace on the front terrace, and a channel of water running along the north edge of the north terrace. Combined with the water in the entry court, it gives the sense that one has tapped an artesian water source. The water surfaces in different subtle ways.

Earth and light, water and fire form the weft of the house.

9

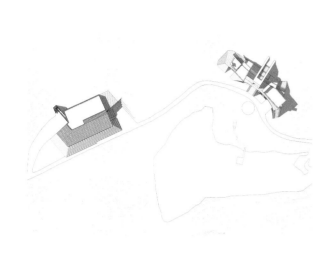

House in a Box Canyon

Set into a box canyon with a north-south axis and abruptly sloping east and west walls, this house is in a sequence of five building pieces. Because of processional nature of the site, each piece acts as a stepping stone to the next: from the arrival gateway, to housing cars, then to the main house, guest house, and meeting lodge. The experience defines an interactive network of spaces.

The site condition for each piece is very different with regard to access to the sun thoughout the day. The trellised and glazed garage/office/pool/greenhouse piece is encountered first. There is an enigmatic quality about the building. As you drive up the canyon, it is on the left—stone terraces as a base for a trellised shell. Adjacent to all that is a big, blank door that goes into the hillside, almost like a munitions storage bunker. It is a mysterious, James Bond-looking entry into the garage. The building is carved into the hillside, into the topography; the lower level is on the grade of the road, and the upper level joins the slope of the hillside. The impression is of a stratified presence, stone strata emerging from the slope and forming a transition to the trellised/glazed cover of the greenhouse. It is a hybrid building. It has dichotomies that are interesting: a frontispiece masking in an intriguing way, hiding, operations that are back in the hillside, and the office perched above all that, looking out, getting morning sun over the greenhouse, and looking toward distant views of a ridge to the southeast.

One hundred yards down the road, is the main house. The strata of the greenhouse/pool piece merge into the hillside, continuing sporadically as a trail of ledges that link to the house. The trail almost goes away, and then begins to reassert itself, coalescing into the base of the house, another stack of stone strata upon which the main living functions of the house are placed.

The base extends the canyon wall. It is almost as if the canyon wall continues, stepping out and down toward the lake, establishing a mesa which is populated with a series of pavilions. There are both above ground and below-ground connections back to the hillside. It is a very

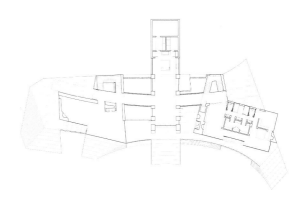

different sense of integration into the landscape from, say, Turtle Creek [pp. 172-199]. There, once you penetrate the "dam" in the foreground, there is a dissolution of mass and an extreme openness to the realm of the site beyond. In this case, there is a penetration into the site, an excavation into the hillside that suggests a surrogate topography. There is an affinity yet an inversion between the two projects.

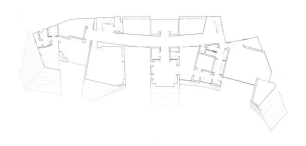

On the honed-granite base are positioned glazed, solar-controlled pavilion-like structures. To the south is the living area; to the north is the master bedroom suite. In the middle of the two pavilions is the family room, a projecting stone penninsula that cuts through and separates the public area from the more private areas. It is an extension of a minor ridge that comes off the hillside perpendicular to the general direction of the topographic contours. It anchors and connects the stone base to the hillside. The house feels very rooted, but there is also a feeling of lightness to the elements on top of the base that are linked together by a long, arcing circulation route that begins at the south as a glazed entry canopy and then continues through the house, defining trellised light zones.

In the base itself are the more sequestered functions like the library and office that, unlike like the spaces on the platform above, don't require an abundance of light. On the west side of the circulation arc, par-alleling it, are zones that bring light to the lower level. Below, there is a sense of the imprint of the circulation arc above.

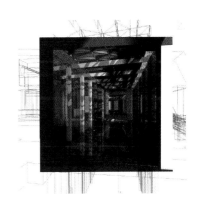

Like Turtle Creek, this house engages the site quite literally, with a similar relation of stone-to-stone. In Dallas it was limestone ledge to limestone substrate. Here it is granite to granite. But there is a very different intention. It is still about stone as a foregrounding element, but here the stone suggests a surrogate canyon wall that acts as a base upon which glazed pavilions, not unlike the lantern-like qualities of the Rosen-thal house in Manhattan Beach, California [pp. 152-169] are placed.

11

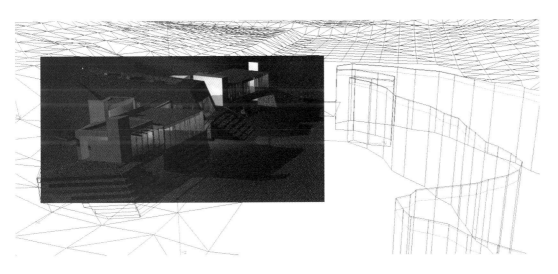

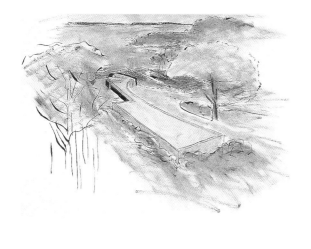

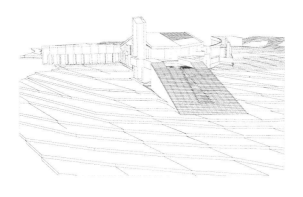

MASSACHUSETTS BAY HOUSE

The site is on Massachusetts Bay. It's a rocky, forested shoreline with an island view in the distance, Marblehead across the bay, Salem to the southwest. As the site plunges down to the ocean, the forest opens up to the shoreline. Passing through a heavily wooded area between the main road and the house, there is a real sense of transition, of psychological deceleration.

The house pivots, in a convex arc, around an enormous beech tree that has drifted away from the forested edge. The house is isolated from the forest and flanked on the extreme east and west edges by outcrops. At the bottom of the site, the house slopes up, like a stone taus in the foreground. Native stone merges with the sloping berms of the house, and the rough stone gathered at the base of the slope *gives way* to a slate roof, as though the stone had been machined from rough to smooth. The house "vignettes" into the ground.

The convex arc of the house receives the arriving visitor and forms a visual barrier to the water, denying the view. But cutting through it is a fissure between the main, living body of the house and the garage/service quarters. The entry fissure is fully glazed, and is focused toward the sea. It is a crystalline realm wedged between the two bodies of the house that provides an immediate connection and view release through the house, even before you go inside. Once inside, the house opens fully to the views.

The house climbs up out of the site, and then tumbles toward the sea. As the stone metamorphoses from rough to smooth, ascending on the entry side, an upper-level loft bedroom area and a double-height living space are generated. Then the house falls down the other way toward the water from the upper, master suite level in stone steps that form a bleacher/terrace with views toward the water.

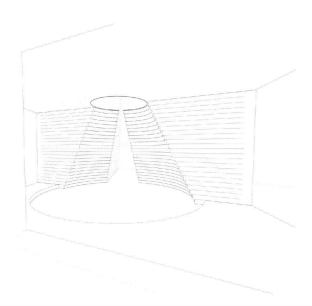

A grotto/spa, housed beneath this stone terrace, receives light from an oculus skylight and has a view aperture that begins as a vertically attenuated, narrow triangular slot within the grotto and fans out to open to the view. Glazed steps complete the alignment of the stone steps on the exterior. There is privacy within the grotto, yet from within one is offered a significant fragment of the panorama of Massachusetts Bay.

There is a stone sea wall that receives the cascading forms of the slope, regularizing and terminating the flow of the site. There are boulders that tumble into the foreground berming on the arrival side, and also bite into the garage and the earth berm.

The double-height fireplace in the main living space frames the procession into the grotto. It is a commanding element that defines and brackets an upper westward-looking terrace outside the master suite. Though elevated, the upper level is like a cave or cliff dwelling, carved into the stone body of the house. There is a weighty aspect, but it is accessed by a glass stair.

The house is about rootedness in site—like so many of my houses—from the tree, to the boulders, to the embracing of the views. It shows a very literal growth from the site—from boulders to finished stone.

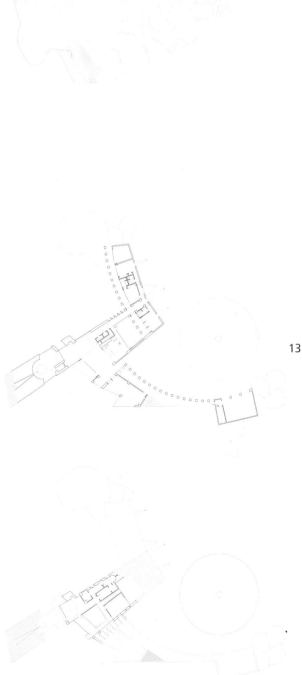

13

LA LUZ

14

On a semi-arid mesa west of the Rio Grande bosque, a close-knit community of townhouses creates intimate private realms while conserving open areas for common view and use. An indoor-outdoor life within each unit is made possible by responding to the spectacular views and natural conditions.

An urban environment and open natural areas can and should coexist, especially in New Mexico. Existing natural patterns should be recognized and reinforced. These factors suggested a concentration of development on the high ground of the site. The massed townhouses recognize particular landscape and view nuances and suggest a man-made escarpment.

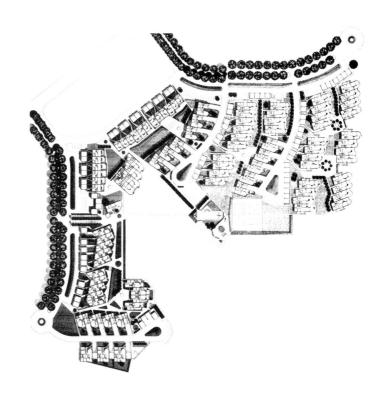

The building forms and materials provide protection from widely varying climatic forces. The massive adobe walls made from materials on the site serve as heat reservoirs and form acoustical barriers. Large glass areas are recessed beneath deep concrete fascias. Some adobe walls are stuccoed white to bounce light into a patio or room.

The earth-engaged houses
face either private cul-de-
sac streets or pedestrian
courts. Glass walls aim east
at mountain and city views.
The west sides of the units
offer a predominantly blank
wall to the impact of the
low afternoon sun and are
closed to the dust-laden
spring winds. The patios
offer shelter from winter
winds, yet act as receptors
for trapping solar radiation.

20

Following the existing contours, the stepped section longitudinally allows view over units below toward river and mountains.

KAMINSKY HOUSE

Albuquerque, New Mexico
1971/**73**

A semi-arid bluff overlooks the Rio Grande and the city to the east with a wall of mountains beyond. The terrain slopes rapidly toward the river.

This economical house for a family of four is adapted to the sloping topography of the site and to the southwestern climate. All areas within the house are oriented toward panoramic views.

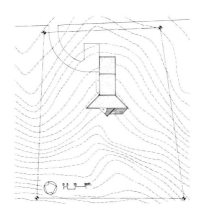

The stepped section of the house relates to the existing slope, generating a one story facade on the west while three levels command panoramic views to the east. The house has essentially blank south and west walls to reduce solar impact on the interior while also buffering dust storms from the same direction. The splayed walls divert winds out and around the east terrace and deck areas.

33

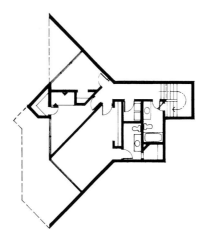

The sleeping zone is on the ground level for privacy, with living and dining and deck areas cantilevered above. A study loft is suspended over the living room and has its own deck.

34

Deep overhangs shelter the east glazing and partially cover the deck areas, which look toward a wall of mountains and the drama of the New Mexico sky.

BOULDER HOUSE

Albuquerque, New Mexico
1975/**76**

40

Sectionally, the house steps down the hillside—roof terraces, a pool and outdoor decks following the sloping topography. The main entry at the east, under the sloping solar roof, falls on a long axis that opens across a covered deck toward the distant view of Mt. Taylor fifty miles away.

Attuned to this particular locale, both passive and active energy strategies shape the architecture. In a region of 360 days of sun and 8 inches of rain per year, these responses are integral to the house with inclined solar collectors, mirroring the slope of the mountain. The thermal mass of the 12-inch thick masonry walls absorbs the heat from the daytime sun and slowly radiates warmth into the interior spaces in the cool of the evening.

The radial masonry fin walls of the living area buffer low west sun angles but permit views toward city lights at night and distant mountains. Large openings frame city views to the southwest and also permit the penetration of afternoon winter sun. Openings are protected from southerly summer sun by overhangs. Outdoor spaces are protected from cold winds by surrounding walls that, in turn, absorb solar radiation to enhance winter use.

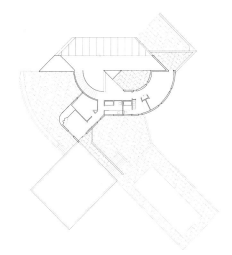

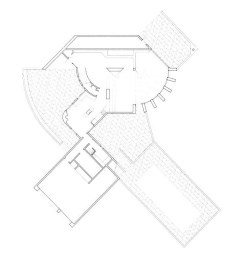

RIO GRANDE VALLEY HOUSE

Albuquerque, New Mexico
1983/**85**

Albuquerque's North Valley is charged with landscape memories. Over time, the widely meandering course of the Rio Grande left a rich residue of agricultural land. Successive waves of Native Americans, Spanish settlers, and emigrants from the eastern United States have lived on and worked this soil, each group leaving its traces.

Sited in this historic area, the house responds gently to the valley ambiance, extending into the alfalfa fields with a horizontality appropriate to the sweep of the valley and the wall of the Sandia Mountains beyond. The house rises softly from the irrigated fields, its anchoring wall concealing the matrix of courtyards within. A rural, North Valley feeling is suggested by the pitched metal roofs, the long, low massive walls, and the promise of inner gardens.

48

The high continuous wall separates the house from the foreground alfalfa fields. Beyond the wall an entry autocourt gives way to a transitional patio, leading to the main entry.

A skewed grid of linear, pavilion-like pieces align mountain views while maintaining the imprint of the orthogonal pattern of surrounding fields. The intersecting pitched roof pavilions guide circulation and double on the east-west axis as a solar greenhouse. Retreating to the cool north side of the house, the sunken living area maintains winter southern exposure via the greenhouse pavilion.

A pool and patio form the centerpiece for the surrounding living, dining, and kitchen pavilions, and shady pergola.

RIO GRANDE VALLEY

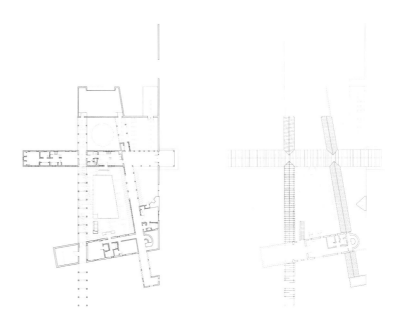

Bedrooms are stacked in a two-story "house" with the upper-level master suite served by a circular stair, contained in a silo-like tower. A master bedroom terrace stair connects back to the central court level. Retreat and respite are enhanced by the inwardly turned, contemplative courtyard plan.

TROY HOUSE

Taos, New Mexico
1983/**85**

Near Taos, on an ancient sagebrush plain, the Troy House rises from the landscape as it recalls the angles of the San Antonio Mountains on the western horizon beyond. The house is a surrogate mountain, an abstraction of the landscape.

In mirroring the slopes of the surrounding mountains, the house ascends from a bermed embankment that anchors the house to the earth's thermal stability to the adjacent spaces. Likewise from the north, a wide stairway ascends, its angled parapet paralleling the mountain angle. On descending the stair, the views are channeled to the snow-capped Truchas Peaks.

A portal-colonnade guides circulation to the house entry as it aligns with a mountain peak on the horizon.

LYNCH HOUSE

Tesuque, New Mexico
1983/**85**

This house, north of Santa Fe, stretches out at the edge of a precipitous drop to a sparsely vegetated slope below. Arrayed like a necklace of varied pieces, the house takes optimum advantage of views and climate. The site, the local design covenants, and the program suggested a hybrid form, a quiet synthesis of vernacular and technology.

The protective hacienda 'type' of northern New Mexico is here broken open and unfurled. The inner core faces south and, from its location on the precipice, surveys a valley and distant mountains. A curvilinear 'defensive' wall is established along the north to block winter wind and to shield the entry—only small openings perforate this wall.

73

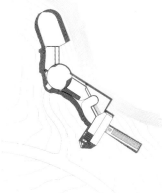

The small, serial views are given a broader framework when one diverges from the linking circulation path to the outdoor areas. These patios are warm, sunlit, socializing areas, which contrast with the cool, shaded arrival face.

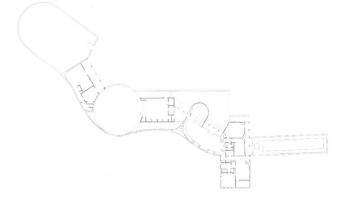

Arrival into the auto court presents a panoramic view, which is then selectively framed and repeatedly revealed as one follows the arcing longitudinal wall.

The dichotomies established between shell and core, between north and south, between formal entry and informal gathering places parallel the extremes of the altiplano of New Mexico. Hard, smooth finishes and soft massive forms agree syntactically in an idiom which acknowledges, extends, and ultimately escapes a literal reliance on the local vernacular.

FULLER HOUSE

Scottsdale, Arizona

This High Sonoran desert site is enclosed by peaks and eroded granite ridges. Below this encircling rim, sparse vegetation, at once hardy and fragile, surrounds the house and speaks of the adaptations necessary for life beneath an unremitting sun.

In this desert environment, architecture, landscape and human procession join in a synchronous dance. The low, weighty perimeter of the house connects in its massiveness and its color to the powerful geologic context. Contrasting brittle steel shade structures create shadow patterns that recall the tracery cast on the site by the lacy branches of the ocotillo and palo verde.

85

The house is axially positioned in relation to the east-west travel of the sun. Daily living patterns shift from morning to evening. A sunrise-viewing pavilion is situated above the breakfast room; an interior 'canyon', a gallery with centered, sequential water system, leads past kitchen and dining fragments as the 'mountain', the pyramidal study, introduces the 'valley', the central courtyard; across the 'valley' a trellised, sunset tower completes the sequence.

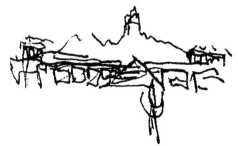

Inside, water issues from a black granite block and runs through a channel parallel to the east-west axis of the house. The water's path culminates in a quiet pool in the courtyard.

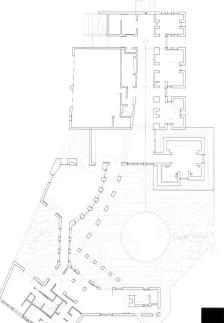

The gentle standoff between built form and a desert environment is expressed in the project as a poetic tension. The line of demarcation between the house and the terrain becomes ambiguous. At certain places the desert enters as boulders tumble into the courtyard.

Refuge in this arid precinct has been created by the presence of water, shade and enclosure. Looking out from this sequestered desert retreat, the majestic landscape and the vast sky become theater.

A significant part of the house is set partially underground providing thermal stability while capturing eye-level views of the desert landscape. The higher vantage points, like the sunset tower, have views across the valley toward nighttime lights of Phoenix, to the sunset in the west, and to the mountains in the east.

ZUBER HOUSE

102

Poised on and excavated into the south-facing slope of Mummy Mountain, this house offers sweeping views of Phoenix and the valley it occupies. In plan, the house forms a T. The vertical leg engages the mountain, while the horizontal arm offers a panoramic view toward the valley.

The north-south "mountain house" is deeply recessed. It is constructed of rough concrete block using a colored aggregate that recalls the color of the mountain face.

The east-west "panoramic house" is a lighter color and projects out from the mountain house. Its stucco finish is the gray-green of the desert floor.

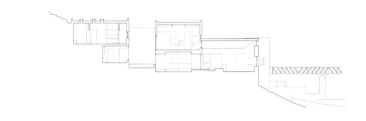

The house contains a sequence of water events, varying from the contemplative to the active. Water descends in gentle steps from the mountain house, where the study-cave contains a silent pool. The water continues over a small cascade to a diagonally rotated pool and, finally, to a channel that leads into the entry space of the house.

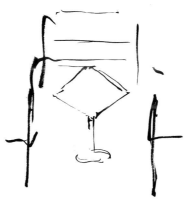

The east-west house forms the major building facade and houses the more public areas of the residence—entry, gallery, living, kitchen and dining. Although the focus of the house is on the outdoors, it is still sensitive to the harsh effects of the Arizona summer sun. The south windows are modestly scaled and recessed into two-foot-thick walls of stucco-covered concrete block. Steel horizontal fins add additional protection.

Isolated above the water realm, the master bedroom suite becomes both private inner sanctum and control tower. In the room, views are framed into the upper pool and gallery, and out to the mountains and city of Phoenix beyond.

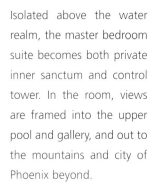

113

Connecting the mountain house and the panoramic house are two masonry towers, rotated to allow raking views of the city in the distance and the valley to the southeast. One tower sprouts a steel bridge that aims diagonally toward the horizon and aligns with local flight patterns.

The skeletal bridge, which angles away, is a gateway for approaching visitors and a focused viewing platform that extends the living area. From its vantage point, one has a clear view of nature's diurnal and seasonal dramas over the Phoenix valley. The limestone paving blocks used inside the house flow outside to become the paving of the bridge. The joints between blocks are left open, allowing light to emanate from below at night. The bridge seems to go nowhere while taking you anywhere.

WINANDY HOUSE

Desert Highlands, Arizona
1988/**91**

The organization of this house in the High Sonoran Desert is influenced by the desert dichotomy—the need to retreat from, and hold back, the harsh desert environment coexists with the desire to open up to desert views. This led to the development of a simple courtyard house transformed at its edges. The outbuildings peel away centrifugally from the tight knit plan of the main house and stretch out to align themselves with the views of high desert ridges, sunset and the lights of Phoenix.

The courtyard is a physical and psychological haven around which all other spaces are organized. The definition between indoor and outdoor space is ambiguous as the courtyard becomes an integral part of the living area.

Quietly circulating water establishes a procession that leads to the pool in the rear court. Cantilevered trusses hover above the inner courtyard wall to allow a ring of daylight to glow at its periphery.

In combination with obscure glass privacy screens, a two-sided fireplace, visible from both sleeping area and study, differentiates the private from the more public zone.

The perforated masonry wall defines a shady loggia which connects the exterior courtyard area with the house interior. Through the apertures in the wall, glimpses are afforded of the courtyard and the ridge beyond.

The ground-borne massing and the materials chosen are of the desert and ultimately, when decomposed, will return to the desert. The zoning-mandated weighty clay tile roof is positioned over a continuous clerestory slot that glows at night, appearing to float above the massive concrete masonry walls.

VENICE HOUSE

Venice, California
1988/**91**

This house turns its back on the interventions in the Los Angeles landscape and focuses instead on the ocean and the thin strip of land that meets it. The house sets up a series of vantage points, some more accessible than others. Rather than the topical, this house deals with the timeless aspect of Los Angeles— the relationship between the land and water.

Tile stairs ascend from the master bedroom terrace to the upper roof terrace "bleachers" and deck to offer views in all directions: ocean, city lights, LAX takeoffs, Palos Verdes, and the Santa Monica mountains. The concrete armature defines an aperture that focuses the ocean view from the bed.

142

On the ocean side, a four-foot thick, poured-in-place concrete armature suggests gigantic bleached bones along the shore. A water-coated granite monolith fronts the public walk along the beach. Evoking geologic strata, it is an urban offering—inviting the passerby's touch.

The red steel window at the end of the entry view axis, 9-feet wide, 13-feet high, and 2,000 pounds, pivots horizontally to open the aperture to the ocean. The wet film on the granite forms a "water to water" visual bridge to the ocean when viewed from within the house.

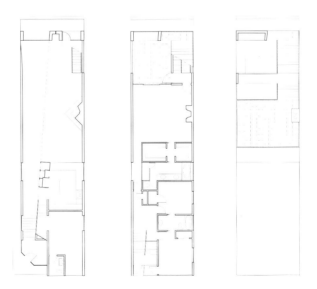

Adjacent to the red-glazed frame is a three-by-seven-by-three-foot subtraction from the concrete armature. In it, running floor to ceiling, is a three-quarter-inch wide by twelve-inch deep fragment of glass that was cast into the concrete pour. Through the glass is a kaleidoscopic view of the ocean, the sky, and the sand.

146

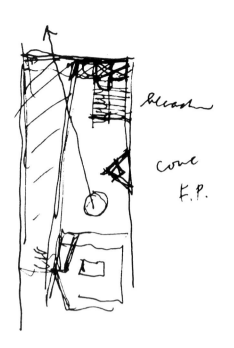

In the entry, the upward sloping ceiling and the divergent lines of the granite "runway" reverse the perspective—space is collapsed, drawing the ocean and horizon toward the viewer. Attention is focused on the ocean and the realms beyond.

Throughout the interior, zones of natural light diffused through obscure glass, create lateral divisions and also render a glowing dimension to the street/entry end.

ROSENTHAL HOUSE

Manhattan Beach, California
1986/**93**

As a home and studio for a toy designer, this house becomes a toy itself—exploratory and climbable, a kind of excavated Rubik's Cube. The displaced cast-in-place concrete foreground piece with its base parallel to the street, seems to have slid from the cubic envelope of the house. The upper terrace of the displaced volume becomes the crossroads of the house.

Positioned in the right angle of a small triangular site, the house forms an "X" in plan with diagonal views to Malibu, Palos Verdes and straight out to the Pacific.

153

The site had been occupied by a deteriorating bungalow—the only element that was retained was a perfect iconic 1950s kidney-shaped swimming pool.

The lower dwelling area, located beneath the upper terrace, and filling the entire square footprint of the cube, opens fully to the courtyard and pool.

Selective views from the upper levels to the courtyard are framed by the outer skin of the excavated cube.

155

The outer stucco shell of the house modulates light, allows ventilation and seizes views to the surrounding area. Inside this enclosure are three distinct levels—the first a living area, the second a studio and the top a "sleeping lantern" clad in moveable translucent glass panels. All of these areas can be accessed via separate internal and external stair systems.

On the second level, the front quarter of the square is cut away, leaving an L-shaped interior around an open terrace. Sloping walls define the terrace and signify a private domain containing the gallery space/studio.

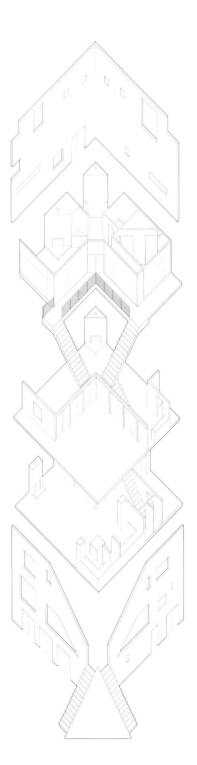

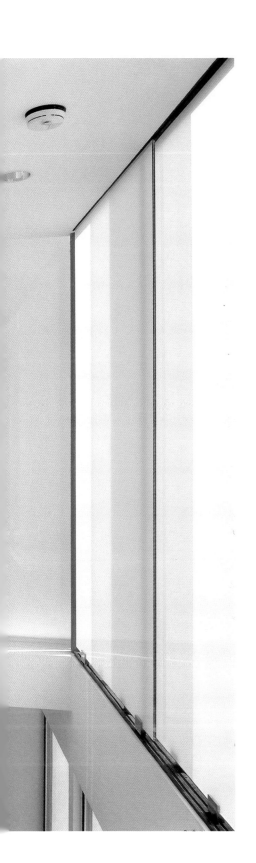

In the master bedroom of the third level, the light intensity is manipulated with sandblasted glass panels, resulting in a subtle modulation. The panels can be overlapped several times creating a dense bottle green or left singular for maximum translucency.

The house both emanates and receives light, while seeing itself in reflection. Its transformability is appropriate as a setting for the development of experimental toys.

TURTLE CREEK HOUSE

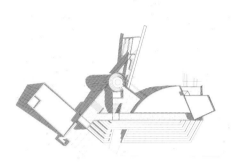

Sited at the convergence of two major continental flyways on the Turtle Creek watershed in Dallas, this house is a response to the client's passion for birdwatching.

In the foreground, anchoring limestone ledges that create a weighty and earthbound dam of expectations. The ledges suggest a timeless relationship to the site, one that has geologic parallels to the Austin Chalk Formation, the spine that runs north-south through Dallas. The occupation by birds is assured by the inclusion of native plants on the ledges.

A central fissure in the ledges, formalized as entry, is the point of departure for access to the many vantage points, poised throughout the house. A central "sky ramp" projects from the fissure into the surrounding canopy of trees. Aimed toward the sky, it touches the ground lightly, allowing the undergrowth to flow beneath it.

As the house reaches out from its earthbound datum, it opens into and explores the various levels of avian habitation: water's edge, understorey, foliage, canopy and sky. The fissure also separates the north and south wings of the house. The north wing is the domain where everyday life unfolds and informal gathering occurs. The south wing is the realm of formal social gathering and for private retreat above.

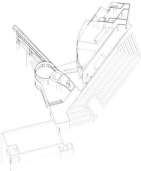

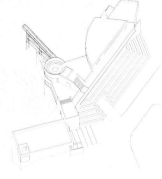

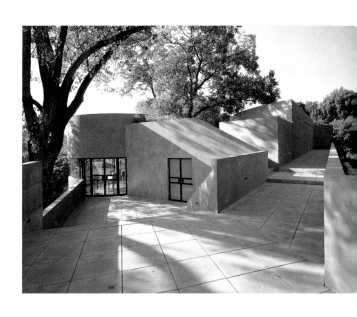

A third zone of the house—the roofscape—engages the sky. From here walkways over the house survey bird habitats, arriving guests and the Dallas skyline. Penetrating the parapet is an intimate rooftop arena both inwardly focusing and providing a "blind"—like shield for outward viewing. The central steel "sky ramp" projects the entry fissure into the canopy of trees and beyond to the sky.

TURTLE CREEK

182

A triangular seating prow which defines a small grassy terrace extends eastward from the dining tower.

A twenty-foot square convex polished stainless steel piece reflects and transforms the house and its surroundings.

The black steel catwalk links the living area, dining tower and sky ramp, and provides a close range encounter with the stainless steel mirror.

The entry fissure in the ledges is a channel that separates the house into north and south "houses." An interior black-steel bridge spans this entry hall. The hall's twenty-foot ceiling reveals the stratified tree canopy outside.

187

The floating wall is an interior counterpoint to the exterior stainless-steel mirror. It hovers above the floor plane of the living room, dissociating itself from the outer walls. It is an object isolated by space and glass from the rest of the house.

190

The arcing glass wall of the living area provides views toward Turtle Creek and its forested margin and, in the winter, distant views of the skyline.

A corner terrace joins living area and library and provides access to the lawn and pathways to Turtle Creek.

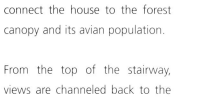

The bedroom and flanking terrace connect the house to the forest canopy and its avian population.

From the top of the stairway, views are channeled back to the entry fissure.

PROJECT CHRONOLOGY

Houses

1970/1971
Predock House and Studio
Albuquerque, New Mexico

1967/1974
La Luz Community
Albuquerque, New Mexico

1971/1973
Kaminsky House
Albuquerque, New Mexico

1975/1976
Boulder House
Albuquerque, New Mexico

1977/1978
Barrow House
Albuquerque, New Mexico

1981/1982
Santa Fe House
Santa Fe, New Mexico

1981/1982
Chernush Addition
Arlington, Virginia

1983
Desert Highlands (project)
Pinnacle Peak, Arizona

1983/1985
Rio Grande Valley House
Albuquerque, New Mexico

1983/1985
Troy House
Taos, New Mexico

1984/1986
Lynch House
Tesuque, New Mexico

1984/1987
Fuller House
Scottsdale, Arizona

1988
Mercer Island Estate (project)
Mercer Island, Washington

1986/1989
Zuber House
Phoenix, Arizona

1988/1991
Winandy House
Desert Highlands, Arizona

1988/1991
Venice House
Venice, California

1993
Massachusetts Bay House (project)
Beverly, Massachusetts

1986/1993
Rosenthal House
Manhattan Beach, California

1987/1993
Turtle Creek House
Dallas, Texas

1999
Strata House (project)
Paradise Valley, Arizona

1999
House in a Box Canyon (project)
Santa Fe, New Mexico

1999/2000
Kaminsky House II
Albuquerque, New Mexico

1999
Lake House (project)
Dallas, Texas

2000/2003
Monterey Bay House
Santa Cruz, California

2000/2002
Shadow House
Santa Fe, New Mexico

AWARDS

Turtle Creek House
Dallas, Texas

Western Home Awards
AIA and *Sunset Magazine*
1997-1998

Honor Award
Western Mountain Region
AIA
1996

Design Ovation
American Society of Interior Designers
1995

Best in Residential Design
Interiors Magazine
1995

Award of Excellence for Design
Architectural Record:
Record Houses
1994

First Place
Excellence in Construction Awards Competition
Associated Builders and Contractors
1994

Award of Excellence
AIA / Albuquerque
1993

Rosenthal House
Manhattan Beach, California

Award of Merit
AIA / Albuquerque
1994

Merit Award
AIA / Cabrillo Chapter
1993

Merit Award
AIA / Los Angeles
1994

Venice House
Venice, California

Honor Award
AIA / California Council
1991

Award of Merit
AIA / Los Angeles
1990

Citation
Western Mountain Region
AIA
1990

Winandy House
Desert Highlands, Arizona

Award for Excellence in Architecture
AIA / New Mexico
1992

Zuber House
Phoenix, Arizona

Award of Excellence for Design
Architectural Record:
Record Houses
1990

Honor Award for Excellence in Architecture
Western Mountain Region
AIA
1990

Fuller House
Scottsdale, Arizona

AIA National Honor Award
1987

Honor Award
Western Mountain Region
AIA
1986

Lynch House
Tesuque, New Mexico

Award for Excellence in Architecture
Western Mountain Region
AIA
1987

Troy House
Taos, New Mexico

Award of Excellence
New Mexico Society of Architects
1987

Award for Excellence in Architecture
Western Mountain Region
AIA
1987

Rio Grande Valley House
Albuquerque, New Mexico

Award of Honor
Western Mountain Region
AIA
1986

Award of Excellence for Design
Architectural Record:
Record Houses
1986

Merit Award
AIA and *Sunset Magazine*
Western Home Awards
1985-1986

Honor Award
New Mexico Society of Architects
1985

Desert Highlands
Pinnacle Peak, Arizona

Citation
Progressive Architecture
Annual Awards Program
1984

Santa Fe House
Santa Fe, New Mexico

Award of Excellence for Design
Architectural Record:
Record Houses
1982

Barrow House
Albuquerque, New Mexico

Merit Award
New Mexico Society of Architects
1982

Boulder House
Albuquerque, New Mexico

Award of Excellence for Design
Architectural Record:
Record Houses
1977

La Luz Community
Albuquerque, New Mexico

25 Year Award of Excellence
AIA / Albuquerque
1993

New Mexico Register of Cultural Properties
1977

Award of Honor
New Mexico Society of Architects
1970

Award of Excellence for Design
Architectural Record:
Record Houses
1970

Raven Townhouse, La Luz Community
Albuquerque, New Mexico

Citation
AIA and *Sunset Magazine*
Western Home Awards
1969-1970

Predock House and Studio
Albuquerque, New Mexico

Merit Award
Western Mountain Region
AIA
1971

SELECTED BIBLIOGRAPHY

Houses

2000

Allen, Isabel. *Structure as Design*. Massachusetts: Rockport Publishers Inc., 2000, 24-29.
TURTLE CREEK HOUSE

Cohen, Edie. *West Coast Rooms*. Massachusetts: Rockport Publishers, Inc., 2000, 120-123.
ROSENTHAL HOUSE

Futugawa, Yukio. *GA Houses 63*. Tokyo, Japan: ADA Edita Tokyo Co., Ltd., March 2000, 150-153.
HOUSE IN A BOX CANYON

1999

Castle, Helen. *Modernism and Modernization in Architecture*. John Wiley and Sons, Ltd., March 1999, front inside cover, 13, 92-99.
TURTLE CREEK HOUSE

Gelernter, Mark. *A History of Buildings in their Cultural American and Technological Context Architecture*. Great Britain: Manchester University Press, July 1999, 315-316.
ZUBER HOUSE

Infanzon, Nestor. "Two Houses in Dallas: A conversation about architecture, art and life," *Texas Architect*, 67-70.
TURTLE CREEK HOUSE

Zabalbeascoa, Anatxu and Javier Rodriguez Marcos. *Antoine Predock: Architecture of the Land*. Barcelona: Gustavo Gili, 1999, 32-41.
TURTLE CREEK HOUSE

Zevon, Susan. *Outside Architecture*. Massachusetts: Rockport Publishers, Inc., September 1999, 12, 64-77.
FULLER HOUSE, ZUBER HOUSE, VENICE HOUSE, ROSENTHAL HOUSE, TURTLE CREEK HOUSE

1998

Boyer, Charles. *Houses by the Sea*. Paris: Telleri, April 1998, 90-97.
VENICE HOUSE

Cerver, Francisco Arsensio. *Architects of the World*. Spain: Whitney Library of Design, 1998, pp.160-163.
ZUBER HOUSE, VENICE HOUSE

Collins, Brad and Elizabeth Zimmermann, eds. *Antoine Predock Architect 2*, New York: Rizzoli International Publications, 1998.

Frampton, Kenneth. *Technology, Place, and Architecture: The Jerusalem Seminar in Architecture*. New York: Rizzoli International Publications, 1998, 224-227, 283.
FULLER HOUSE, VENICE HOUSE, TURTLE CREEK HOUSE

Lyon, Hortense. *American Contemporary Houses*. Paris: Telleri, September 1998, 70-79.
ZUBER HOUSE

Pearsman, Hugh. *Contemporary World Architecture*. London, England: Phaidon Press Limited, 1998, 18-19, 48-50, 62, 78, 94, 224, 227, 241, 291, 330, 339-343.
ZUBER HOUSE

1997

Architecture Today, Phaidon Press Ltd., 1997, 110, 120-125, 128, 242, 265.
ZUBER HOUSE, VENICE HOUSE

Baker, Geoffrey. *Antoine Predock, Architectural Monograph No. 49*. London: Academy Editions, 1997.

Dixon, John Morris. "Due Recognition," *Harvard Design Magazine*, Summer 1997, 54.
LA LUZ

Doubilet, Susan and Boles, Daralice. *American House Now: Contemporary Architectural Directions*. New York: Universe Publishing, 1997, 13, 110-120.
FULLER HOUSE

Gregory, Daniel. "Nature Gallery," *Sunset Magazine*, October 1997, 108.
TURTLE CREEK HOUSE

JaeHong, Lee. *Antoine Predock Architect Monograph* Korea: Korean Architect, 1997.

Loomis, John. *Dictonnaire de l'Architecture Moderne et Contemporaine*. Paris: Editions, 1997, 728-729.

Pendergast, Sara. ed. *Contemporary Designers*. New York: St. James Press,1997, 682-685.

Predock, Antoine. *One House Series: Turtle Creek House*. New York: The Monacelli Press, 1997.
TURTLE CREEK HOUSE

"Progressive Architecture Awards," *Architecture*, January 1997, 60-99.

1996

Cerver, Francisco Asensio. *Architectural Houses 01*. Barcelona: Atrium International, 1996, 98-107.
VENICE HOUSE

Devido, Alfredo, FAIA. *House Design: Art and Practice*, John Wiley and Sons, Inc., March 1996, 68-69, 100-101.
LA LUZ, FULLER HOUSE

Filler, Martin. "Surveying a Century," *House Beautiful*, November 1996, 134.
RIO GRANDE VALLEY HOUSE

Ghirardo, Diane. *Architecture After Modernism*. London: Thames and Hudson Ltd., 1996, cover, 79-82.
WINANDY HOUSE

Hess, Alan. *Hyperwest: American Residential Architecture on the Edge*. New York: Whitney Library of Design, 1996, 54-55, 74-77.
FULLER HOUSE, ZUBER HOUSE

Keln, Tereas. *Architektura Ziemi*. Warsaw, Poland: Murator, 1996, 100-101, 116.
LA LUZ

Kessler, Brad. "Great Walls of Fire," *House and Home*, November/December 1996, 27.
ZUBER HOUSE

LeBlanc, Sydney. *Whitney Guide to 20th Century American Architecture: A Travelers Guide to 220 Key Buildings*. New York: Watson-Gupthill, 1996, cover, 191, 195, 197.
VENICE HOUSE

Pearson, Clifford A. *Modern American Houses*. New York: McGraw Hill, 1996, 116-119, 142-143.
LA LUZ, BOULDER HOUSE

Reis, Michael. "Interview—Antoine Predock," *Contemporary Design*, Winter 1996, Volume 2, No. 1, 46-57.
VENICE HOUSE, TURTLE CREEK HOUSE

1995

"The AD 100 Designers and Architects," *Architectural Digest*, September 1995, 112.
TURTLE CREEK HOUSE

Crosbie, Michael J., "Why Can't Johnny Size a Beam," *Progressive Architecture*, June 1995, 95.
FULLER HOUSE

DellaFlora, Anthony. "Celebrity Architect Gets Triple Whammy," *Albuquerque Journal*, April 2, 1995, D12.

"Dialogo Con la Naturaleza," *Buenos Aeries La Nacion-Architectura*, June 21, 1995.
TURTLE CREEK HOUSE

Dietsch, Deborah. "Predock's Example," *Architecture*, March 1995, 15.

Dillon, David. "American Visionary," *Architecture*, March 1995, 55-93.

Frampton, Kenneth and David Larkin. *American Masterworks: The 20th Century House*. New York: Rizzoli International Publications, 1995, 272-281.
FULLER HOUSE

Fuchigami, Masayuki. "Contemporary Architects—Ideas and Works," *Cross Currents*, 1995, 170-173.
LA LUZ, VENICE HOUSE, ROSENTHAL HOUSE

Goldberger, Paul. "Architecture: Antoine Predock—Variations on a Cube in Southern California," *Architectural Digest*, March 1995, 110-119.
ROSENTHAL HOUSE

————. "Houses as Art," *The New York Times Magazine*, March 12, 1995, 46-47.
TURTLE CREEK HOUSE

Gorman, Jean. "Best in Residential Design," *Interiors Magazine*, January 1995, 102-103.
TURTLE CREEK HOUSE

Ojeda, Oscar Riera. *The New American House*. New York: Whitney Library of Design, 1995, 88-95.
TURTLE CREEK HOUSE

Predock, Antoine. *Architectural Journeys*, New York: Rizzoli International Publications, 1995.

Sicuso, Arq. Francisco. "Antoine Predock y sus Juegos Geometricos," *La Prensa*, March 6, 1995, 6.
ROSENTHAL HOUSE

"Trails of the Imagination, Part II," *New Mexico Designer Builder Magazine*, July 1995, 5-11.
ZUBER HOUSE

Welsh, John. *Modern House*. London: Phaidon Press Limited, 1995, 48-55.
ZUBER HOUSE

Whiteson, Leon. "Through the looking glass," *Architecture*, March 1995, 125-129.
ROSENTHAL HOUSE

1994

Anderson, Kurt. "Architecture: Antoine Predock, Serious Modernism in Dallas," *Architectural Digest*, March 1994, 104-111.
TURTLE CREEK HOUSE

Architecture, History and Memory" in *The Jerusalem Seminar in Architecture*, Jeruselum: Yad Hanadiv: November 1994, 28-31.

Architectural Record: Record Houses, April 1994, 76-83.
TURTLE CREEK HOUSE

Contemporary Architects-Ideas and Works." *Cross Currents*,1994, 170-173.
LA LUZ, VENICE HOUSE, ROSENTHAL HOUSE

Dillon, David. "Theater of the Trees," *The Dallas Morning News*, February 13, 1994, C1, C10.
TURTLE CREEK HOUSE

Fuchigami, Masayuki. "Antoine Predock—Architect on the Scene," *Kenchiku Bunka*, February 1994, Volume 49, No. 568, 5-7.
LA LUZ, ZUBER HOUSE, VENICE HOUSE

GA Houses 40. Tokyo: A.D.A. EDITA Tokyo Co., Ltd., January 1994, 100-111.
WINANDY HOUSE

GA Houses 42. Tokyo: A.D.A. EDITA Tokyo Co., Ltd., June 1994, 68-93.
ROSENTHAL HOUSE, TURTLE CREEK HOUSE

Collins, Brad and Juliette Robbins. eds. *Antoine Predock Architect*, New York: Rizzoli International Publications, 1994.

Kroloff, Reed. "La Luz: Quarter-Century Accord With Nature," *Phoenix Home and Garden*, February 1994, 40-43.
LA LUZ

Predock, Antoine. "New Visions for Old Age—Airstream Nomads,"*Architecture*, October 1994, 90.

Simon, Morley S. "13 Projects win AIA Awards," *L.A. Architect*, December 1994, 1, 8, 9.
ROSENTHAL HOUSE

"Top 10 Best Design of 1993," *Time*, January 3, 1994, 72.
TURTLE CREEK HOUSE

Webb, Michael. *Architects' Guide to Los Angeles*. San Francisco: The Understanding Business, 1994.
VENICE HOUSE

1993

"Antoine Predock: Haus Und Landschaft," *Hauser*, March 1993, 11.
RIO GRANDE VALLEY HOUSE

Betsky, Aaron. "World in Motion: Architect Antoine Predock Choreographs L.A.," *L.A. Weekly*, June 18-24, 1993, 30-31.

Forgey, Benjamin. "Albuquerque, In Its Own Place," *The Washington Post*, April 10, 1993.

GA Houses 37. Tokyo: A.D.A. EDITA Tokyo Co., Ltd., March 1993, 114-115.
MASSACHUSETTS BAY HOUSE

Jodidio, Philip. *Contemporary American Architects*. Germany: Benedikt Taschen, 1993, 141-151.
ZUBER HOUSE

Man, Martha. "Happy 25th—La Luz Shines at Gala," *Albuquerque Journal*, September 12, 1993, D1, D3.
LA LUZ

New Mexico Business Journal, September 12, 1993, 74-75.
WINANDY HOUSE

Soucek King, Carol. *Empowered Spaces*. New York: PBC International, Inc.,1993, 40-43.
PREDOCK HOUSE AND STUDIO

W Magazine, March 29 - April 5, 1993, 13.

1992

The American House: Design For Living. Washington D.C. and Australia: AIA Press and The Images Publishing Group, 1992, 44-45.
VENICE HOUSE

Antoniades, Anthony C. *Epic Space: Towards the Roots of Western Architecture*. New York: Van Nostrand Reinhold, 1992, 56, 151.
DESERT HIGHLANDS

The Architect's Sketchbook: Current Practice. Exhibition Catalog, Montreal: Centre Canadien d'Architecture, 1992, pp.16-17.

Architectural Houses, Ediciones Atrium SA, 1992, "Inverted Perspective."
VENICE HOUSE

Collyer, Stanley. "Antoine Predock," *Competitions*, Volume 2, Winter 1992, 50-61.

Grenier, Cynthia. "America's 'Outlaw' Architect," *The World and I*, October 1992, 182-187.

Gustmann, Kurt. "Antoine Predock: Die Groben Architekten," *Hauser*, April 1992, 59-70.

Horn, Miriam. "The Rise of the Desert Rat," *Vanity Fair*, March 1992, 112-122.

Marinelli, Janet and Robert Kourik. "Climate and Site," *The Naturally Elegant Home Environmental Style*, 1992, 17.
LA LUZ

Mass, Spring 1992, "An Interview", 22-26.

NZZ Folio, May 1992.
ZUBER HOUSE

Price, V.B. *A City at the End of the World*. Albuquerque: V.B. Price, 1992, 33-35, 75, 78, 85, 92-93.
LA LUZ

Sarzabal, Hernan Barbero. "Oasis abstracto-Una casa en el desierto de Arizona," *El Cronista-Arquitectura and Diseno*, August, 1992, Front cover, 1, 8.
ZUBER HOUSE

"Six International Architects Discuss Their Design Approaches to Integrating Houses into the Natural Environment,"*Architectural Digest*, September 1992, 48.
TROY HOUSE

Webb, Michael. "Architecture: Antoine Predock, Desert Forms Define an Arizona Residence," *Architectural Digest*, March 1992, 142-149, 194.
WINANDY HOUSE

———. "Architettura: Antoine Predock, Scabre geometrie nel paesaggio estremo del deserto," *Architectural Digest*, Italian Edition, April 1992, 152-159, 242.
WINANDY HOUSE

1991

Architectural Digest: The AD 100 Architects. New York: Architectural Digest Publishing Corp., 1991, 188-189.
TROY HOUSE, VENICE HOUSE

Architectural Houses 5: Houses by the Sea. Barcelona: Ediciones Atrium S.A., 1991, 228-236.
VENICE HOUSE

Architectural Houses 9: Houses in the Mountains. Barcelona: Ediciones Atrium S.A., 1991, 120-129.
ZUBER HOUSE

Betsky, Aaron. "On A Roll," *L.A. Times Magazine*, November 17, 1991, 48.

Boissiere, Olivier. "Antoine Predock: Architect of the West," *Vogue Decoration*, February/March 1991, 53-61.
ZUBER HOUSE

Dermansky, Ann. "When Windows Look Their Best," *Elle Decor*, August 1991, 86-97.
VENICE HOUSE

Dibar, Carlos and Diego Armando. "Antoine Predock: Filtrando imagenes," *Arquitectura e Urbanismo, Brazil*, February/March 1991, 36-49.
FULLER HOUSE, VENICE HOUSE

Dillon, David. "Border Crossings," *Architecture*, August 1991.

Dixon, John Morris. "Transcendence on the Beach," *Progressive Architecture*, April 1991, 92-95.
VENICE HOUSE

El Cronista Comercial Arquitectura Construccion, May 1991.
FULLER HOUSE, VENICE HOUSE

GA Houses 31. Tokyo: A.D.A. EDITA Tokyo Co., Ltd., March 1991, 59-61.
ROSENTHAL HOUSE

GA Houses 32. Tokyo: A.D.A. EDITA Tokyo Co., Ltd., July 1991, 116-125.
ZUBER HOUSE

Horn, Miriam. "A Master of Contradictions," *Graphis*, November/December 1991, 80-87.
FULLER HOUSE, VENICE HOUSE

———. "Designing in Hues of Green," *U.S. News & World Report*, February 25, 1991, 58-59.
LA LUZ

Johnson, Jory and Felice Frankel. *Modern Landscape Architecture: Redefining the Garden*. New York: Abbeville Press, 1991, 131-141.
FULLER HOUSE

St. John, David and Antoine Predock, *Terraces of Rain: An Italian Sketchbook*. Santa Fe: Recursos Press, 1991.

Sainz, Jorge. "Con el mar en el salon, casa en la playa, Venice," *A&V* (Monographias de Arquitectura & Vivenda), November-December 1991, 38-41.
VENICE HOUSE

Sarzabal, Hernan Barbero. "Mas Alla Del Limite: Una Casa En Venice, California," *El Cronista Comercial: Arquitectura and Construcción*, March 1991, 1, 4-5.
VENICE HOUSE

World Residential Design 02. Japan: N.I.C. Ltd., 1991, 2, 6-9, 17-28.
ZUBER HOUSE

1990
American Architecture of the 1980s. Washington D.C. The American Institute of Architects Press, 1990, 248-253.
FULLER HOUSE

Boissiere, Olivier. "Antoine Predock: L'Homme de L'Ouest," *L'Architecture d'Aujourd'hui*, October 1990, 177-187.
LA LUZ, ZUBER HOUSE

Campbell, Robert. "Arquitectura: Antoine Predock," *Architectural Digest Spain*, June 1990, 72-79.
LYNCH HOUSE

GA Houses 28. Tokyo: A.D.A. EDITA Tokyo Co., Ltd., March 1990, 67-69.
WINANDY HOUSE, TURTLE CREEK HOUSE

GA Houses 30. Tokyo: A.D.A. EDITA Tokyo Co., December 1990, 118-121.
VENICE HOUSE

Goldberger, Paul. "Drawing the Past is Like Describing an Elephant," *The New York Times*, October 7, 1990.

Lavin, Sylvia. "Dynamics of Venice Beach," *Architectural Digest*, December 1990, 120-123, 218.
VENICE HOUSE

————. "Power to Heal," *Elle Decor*, June/July 1990, 80-88.
ZUBER HOUSE

Lemos, Peter, "Albuquerque architect Antoine Predock marries houses and milieu" *Confetti*, 1990, premier issue, vol. 1, no. 1, 20-22.
FULLER HOUSE

Mulard, Claudine. "D'Adobe et de Stuc," *Architecture Interieure Cree*, February 1990, 100-103.
RIO GRANDE VALLEY HOUSE

Posner, Ellen. "Media and Architecture," *Quaderns*, #184, 1990, 24-29.

————. "We Are In The Desert," *Landscape Architecture*, August 1990, 42-45.
FULLER HOUSE

Stein, Karen D. "Raising Arizona," *Architectural Record: Record Houses,* Mid-April 1990, 88-95.
ZUBER HOUSE

1989-1990
Mulard, Claudine. "Antoine Predock," *Architecture Interieure Crée*, December 1989/January 1990.

1989
"Antoine Predock: Un caso d'inclusività sintetica," *L'Architettura*, March 1989, pp.178-198.

Black Warrior Review. Tuscaloosa: The University of Alabama, 1989, 49.

Farnsworth, Christina. "A 'Dream Mystic' Makes His Mark on Architecture," *Professional Builder*, Mid-October 1989, 17-22.
FULLER HOUSE, VENICE HOUSE

Hart Wright, *Sylvia. Sourcebook of Contemporary American Architecture: From Postwar to Post modern*. New York: Van Nostrand Reinhold, 1989, 103.
LA LUZ

"In Progress—Five Houses," *Progressive Architecture*, June 1989, 43-46.
ZUBER HOUSE, WINANDY HOUSE, VENICE HOUSE, ROSENTHAL HOUSE, TURTLE CREEK HOUSE

Playspaces: Architecture for Children. Exhibition catalog, Des Moines, Iowa: Des Moines Art Center, 1989, 41-47.
FULLER HOUSE

Plummer, Henry. *The Potential House: Three Centuries of American Dwelling*. Tokyo: a + u Publishing Co., September 1989, 244-257.
FULLER HOUSE

Sacchi, Livio. *Il Disegno dell'Architettura Americana*. Rome: Editori Laterza and Figli, 1989, 274-277.
DESERT HIGHLANDS, RIO GRANDE VALLEY HOUSE, FULLER HOUSE

1988
Anderson, Kurt. "An Architect for the New Age," *Time*, April 11, 1988, 72.

"Antoine Predock," *a + u, Japan*, November 1988, 75-130.

Campbell, Robert. "Antoine Predock: Redefining the Traditional Hacienda Near Santa Fe," *Architectural Digest*, April 1988, 18-23.
LYNCH HOUSE

Dillon, David. "Regionalism, But With Many Inventive Twists," *Architecture*, July 1988, 84-87.
LYNCH HOUSE

Lemos, Paul. "Antoine's Altered States," *London Sunday Times Magazine*, June 19, 1988, 76-77.
FULLER HOUSE

Places, Vol. 5, Number 1. Cambridge: The MIT Press, 1988, 54-56.

1987-1988
Price, V.B. "Antoine Predock, FAIA," *Artspace*, Winter 1987-88, 70-78.

1987
"1987 AIA Honor Awards," *Architectural Record*, June 1987, 72-75.
FULLER HOUSE

Burba, Nora and Paula Panich. *The Desert Southwest*. New York: Bantam Books, 1987, 6-7, 66-79.
TROY HOUSE

Center: A Journal for Architecture in America, Vol. 3. Austin: Center for the Study of American Architecture, School of Architecture, The University of Texas at Austin, 1987, 99, 127.
FULLER HOUSE

Dixon, James Morris. "Big Name Architects," *Architecture, Progressive Architecture,* December 1987, 9.

Freeman, Allen. "Forms As Rugged As Their Desert Setting," *Architecture*, May 1987, 128-133.
FULLER HOUSE

GA Houses Special 2: The Emerging Generation in U.S.A. Tokyo: A.D.A. EDITA Tokyo Co., Ltd., November 1987, 52-55.
ZUBER HOUSE

House Beautiful, January 1987, "New Mexico Sanctuary," 70-73.
RIO GRANDE VALLEY HOUSE

The Inhabited Landscape. Exhibition catalog. New York: The Architectural League of New York, 1987.
FULLER HOUSE

Morris, Roger. "Architecture: Antoine Predock," *Architectural Digest*, August 1987, 90-97, 115.
TROY HOUSE

Rasch, Horst. "Komfortable Bleibe in Unwirt Licher Umgebung," *Hauser*, April 1987, 104-111.
FULLER HOUSE

1986
Adams, Robert M. "Desert Spirit," *House & Garden*, December 1986, 132-141, 202-204.
FULLER HOUSE

Anderson, Grace. "Landscape Memories," *Architectural Record: Record Houses*, Mid-April 1986, 72-79.
RIO GRANDE VALLEY HOUSE

Center: A Journal for Architecture in America, Vol. 2. Austin: Center for the Study of American Architecture, School of Architecture, The University of Texas at Austin, 1986, 106-107.
RIO GRANDE VALLEY HOUSE

Crosbie, Michael. "'Vibrant' Italian Sketches," *Architecture*, January 1986, 23.

"House in Albuquerque, USA," *Baumeister*, December 1986, 32-35.
RIO GRANDE VALLEY HOUSE

1985
Annual Exhibition Catalog, American Academy in Rome, 1985, 20-21.
LYNCH HOUSE

Predock, Antoine. *Italian Sketchbooks*. Rome: National Endowment for the Arts Advanced Design Fellowship at the American Academy in Rome, 1985.

1984
"Desert Highlands," *Progressive Architecture*, 31st Annual P/A Awards, January 1984, 126-128.
DESERT HIGHLANDS

"Edelstein mit neuem Schliff," *Hauser*, April 1984, 116-123.
BARROW HOUSE

"In Progress—Four Residences," *Progressive Architecture*, December 1984, 33-35.
RIO GRANDE VALLEY HOUSE, FULLER HOUSE

"La Luz-Stadt In Der Sonne," *Hauser*, March 1984, 254-261.
LA LUZ

Triglyph. Tempe: College of Architecture and Environmental Design, Arizona State University, Fall 1984, 24-27.
DESERT HIGHLANDS

1982
McCoy, Esther and Barbara Goldstein. *Guide to U.S. Architecture 1940-1980*. Santa Monica: Arts + Architecture Press, 1982, 122.
LA LUZ

Portfolio, "In Touch with the Earth," 109, May-June 1982.
LA LUZ

1981
Des Architectures De Terre. Paris: Centre Georges Pompidou/CCI, 1981, 146-147, 178-181.
LA LUZ

Down to Earth. New York: Facts on File, Inc., 1981, 146-147, 178-181.
LA LUZ

Eaton, Ruth. "Mud: An Examination of Earth Architecture," *Architectural Review*, October 1981, 222-229.
LA LUZ

H (Review de l'Habitat Social), France, "L'Example de 'La Luz.'" September 1981, 36-37.
LA LUZ

Kidder-Smith, G.E. with The Museum of Modern Art, New York. *The Architecture of the United States, Volume 3*. New York. Anchor Press/Doubleday, 1981, 512-513.
LA LUZ

Oliver, Richard, ed. *The Making of an Architect: 1881-1981*. New York: Rizzoli International Publications, Inc., 1981, 232.
LA LUZ

1980
'Post-Modernists: Out of the Glass Box," *Forbes Magazine Arabic Issue*, Annual 1980, 19-22.
LA LUZ

1979
Decorative Art and Modern Interiors: Themes in Nature. New York: William Morrow and Company, Inc., 1979, 66-73.
BOULDER HOUSE

Kendall Thompson, Elisabeth. *Houses of the West*. New York: McGraw-Hill, Inc., 1979, 36-37.
BOULDER HOUSE

Miller, Nory. "Kaleidoscope: A Brief Look at Some Other

Recent Buildings of Note," *2nd Annual Review of New American Architecture*, 1979, 146-148.
BOULDER HOUSE

1978
Casa Vogue, Italy, April 1978.
BOULDER HOUSE

Gropp, Louis. *Solar Houses: 48 Energy Saving Designs*. New York: Conde Nast Publications, Inc., 1978, 62-65.
BOULDER HOUSE

1977
Gordon, Barclay F. "Record Houses of 1977," *Architectural Record: Record Houses*. 1977, 60-61.
BOULDER HOUSE

L'Industria Delle Costruzioni, November, 1977, "Casa Monofamiliare nel nuovo Messico," 66-69.
BOULDER HOUSE

Nikkei Architecture, Japan, August 1977.
BOULDER HOUSE

Plumb, Barbara. *Houses Architects Live In*. New York: The Viking Press, 1977, 32-35.
PREDOCK HOUSE AND STUDIO

A View of Contemporary World Architects. Japan: Shinkenchiku-Sha, 1977, 260.

1974
"Kaminsky House," *a + u, Japan*, June 1974, 14-15.
KAMINSKY HOUSE

"Predock House Remodel, Sutin House" *a + u Japan*, April 1974, 61-67.
PREDOCK HOUSE AND STUDIO

"Regionalism: The Southwest," *Progressive Architecture*, March 1974, 60-69.
LA LUZ, KAMINSKY HOUSE

1972
Plumb, Barbara. "Remodeled Compound for Home and Work," *American Home*, November 1972, 112-115.
PREDOCK HOUSE AND STUDIO

Wagner Green, Lois. "Inner City Design For Living," *Interiors*, March 1972, 105-109.
PREDOCK HOUSE AND STUDIO

1971
Davidson, Marshall B. *American Heritage History of Notable American Houses*. New York: American Heritage Publishing Co., Inc., 1971, 52-53.
LA LUZ

Peter, John. "The De-escalation of Dr. Gerber," *Look Magazine*, June 15, 1971, 74-76.
LA LUZ

Predock, Antoine. "La Luz, Albuquerque, N.M.," *Architecture D'Aujourd'hui*, September 1971, 70-73.
LA LUZ

1970
MacMasters, Dan. "La Luz: New Town for Old Albuquerque," *L.A. Times Home Magazine*, June 28, 1970, 14-17, 26.
LA LUZ

Smith, Herbert L., Jr. *Architectural Record: Record Houses of 1970*, Mid-May 1970, 92-93.
LA LUZ

Spiers, Marcia. "City of Adobe and Light," *American Home*, March 1970, 49-55.
LA LUZ

1969
"In NM, Streetside Gardens, A Landscaped Mall," *Sunset Magazine*, November 1969, 105.
LA LUZ

"La Luz-Albuquerque, NM," *New Mexico Architecture*, July/August 1969.
LA LUZ

"La Luz," *Architectural Forum*, July 1969, 65-70.
LA LUZ

"La Luz, Ensemble d'Habitation dans le Desert du Nouveau-Mexique," *L'Architecture Francaise*, France, November/December 1969, 40-42.
LA LUZ

PHOTO CREDITS

Mary Elkins

MODELS IN FOREWARD
p. 10
p. 12
p. 13

Elliott Erwitt

BOULDER HOUSE
p. 40 lower left

Joshua Friewald

LA LUZ
p. 14 upper left
p. 16 lower
p. 17 center
p. 21 lower

KAMINSKY HOUSE
pp. 30-31
pp. 33-37

BOULDER HOUSE
pp. 38-39
p. 40 upper left
pp. 42-43
p. 44 lower
pp. 45-47

Scott Frances/Esto

TURTLE CREEK HOUSE
pp. 188-189
pp. 192-193
p. 196 lower left
p. 197 lower right

Jerry Goffe

LA LUZ
p. 15 center
p. 16 upper left
p. 19 lower
p. 21 upper left

Stephen Green-Armytage

LA LUZ
p. 19 upper right
p. 21 upper right
p. 25 upper right
p. 27 center

Timothy Hursley

LA LUZ
p. 24 center
p. 25 lower
p. 26 center right

RIO GRANDE VALLEY HOUSE
pp. 50-54
p. 56 upper left
pp. 57-59

FULLER HOUSE
pp. 82-101

ZUBER HOUSE
pp. 102-105
pp. 107-112
p. 114 center
p. 115 lower left
p. 116
pp. 118-121

VENICE HOUSE
p. 138 lower left
pp. 142-149
p. 150 upper right
p. 151 center

ROSENTHAL HOUSE
p. 155 upper right
pp. 156-161
p. 165 center right
pp. 166-167
p. 168 lower left
p. 169 center

TURTLE CREEK HOUSE
p.175 center
pp 182-183
pp. 185-186
p. 190 upper right
p. 191 center
p 197 upper right

Mary Nichols

VENICE HOUSE
pp. 139-141

ROSENTHAL HOUSE
pp. 152-154
p. 155 lower right
pp. 162-164
p. 165 upper right
p. 168 upper
pp. 170-171

Antoine Predock

LA LUZ
p. 26 upper left

Kaminsky House
p. 32 center

Robert Reck

TROY HOUSE
pp. 60-69

LYNCH HOUSE
pp. 70-81

ZUBER HOUSE
p. 106 center
p. 113 lower right
p. 117 center

WINANDY HOUSE
pp.122-137

TURTLE CREEK HOUSE
pp.172-174
pp. 176-181
p. 184 center
p. 187 upper right
p. 190 lower left
pp. 194-195
pp. 198-199

STUDIO

1967/**2000**

Geoffrey Adams
Jon R. Anderson**
D. Joseph Andrade
A. Anthony Anella
Jill J. Annarino
Jarrod R. Arellano
Claude Armstrong
Matthew Baird
Sunil R. Bald
Nanci Baldwin
Derrick D. Ballard
Francisco R. Banogon
Victoria Baran
Joseph K. Barden, Jr.
John W. Bass
Geoffrey A. Beebe*
Donald C. Bennett
Grant D. Bennett
Kasha Booraaytee Berry
Timothy Bicknell
Stuart G. Blakely
Marcus A. Blasi
Sarah Jane Borch
Kathleen M. Bost
Stephen C. Boston
Gail Boyer
John C. Brittingham
Ann Bromberg
Mark L. Bruzan
Luke Bulman
Jorge R. Burbano
Patty Burling
Christopher L. Calott
Kathleen Campbell
Leslie A. Campbell
Judith L. Carroll
Michele Marie Caruthers
Phyllis Cece
Kathleen Chambers
Kameron D. Cheney
Sandra L. Cheromiah
Ned Cherry
Michael T. Chin
Deanna Lynn Chino
Linda M. Christensen
Terrance Cisco
April M. Clark
Michele A. Cohen
Devendra N. Contractor*
Laura Cooper
Arthur Thomas Corsie
Dean P. Cowdrey
Peter B. DeJong
Shawn J. Delisio
Mark T. DePree
Eileen Devereux
Angela E. Dirks
Dan Dixson
Mark K. Donahue**
G. Donald Dudley, Jr.
Betty Marie Duffy
Ronald J. Duhamel
Edward Eeds
Raouf El-Beleidy

Treveston R. Elliott
Cameron C. Erdmann
W. Anthony Evanko**
Juan P. Fabres
Beth Ann Farley
Mischa L. Farrell
Paul A. Fehlau
Glen Fellows
Madonna Fernando
Derek S. Fisher
John D. Fleming
Ira Frazin
Alberto I. Frias
Douglas L. Friend**
Jon Van Gaasbeek
Curtis Garcia
Steve R. Gates
Bertrand J. Genoist
Patrick W. Giannini
Allene Gibson
Van H. Gilbert**
Paul L. Gonzales
Arturo G. Griego
Pantaj Gupta
Lorraine Guthrie
Gabriella Frances Gutierrez
Reginalda Gutierrez
Cathy C. Hahn
Pamela Harling
Sanna M. Harma
Regina Lynn Harris*
Robert Mark Harris
Charles W. Hellwig
Susan K. Higdon
Graham F. Hogan
J. Craig Holdren
Nicholas T. Homann
James R. Horn
Katharine E. Howe
David A. Hrabal
C. Aron Idoine
Rebecca A. Ingram
Hiroyuki Isobe
Ronald J. Jacob**
Jennifer Jardine
Irene G. Jimenez
James C. Johnson
Marni Johnson
Janet R. Johnston
Doris C. Kang
Peter F. Karsten
Jocelyn F. Kasero
Kevin Kellogg
Jane Frances King
Karen Jean King
Georgina J. Kish
Kenji J. Kondo
William Konopik
Pamela Ku
Peter J. Lagomarsino
Mark B. Lawton
Matthew R. Lawton
Jennifer M. Lein
Andrea Lenardin Madden

Karen T. Lente
Lawrence Licht**
Scott Alan Lindenau
Armando Lopez
Jose G. Lopez
Gregory S. Lynn
Daniel G. Macias
Pedro A. Marquez
Steven R. Maurice
Karole Mazeika
Cara McCulloch-Lieuwen
Cassandra McDuffie
Robert F. McElheney
Ann McLaughlin
R. Lawrence Mead
Romeo Ilejay Medina, Jr.
C. Courtney Mercer
Kim Miller
David P. Mishler
Edward George Mitchell
Snow Moore
Stanley G. Moore**
Marcia Morris
John J. Morrow
Catherine Mullinax-Jones
Nancy E. Naphcys
A. David Nelson
George Newlands
Elizabeth Nicewander
Timothy W. Nichols
Gary Nolen
Luella Noles
Norman Noonan
Darrell Brett Oaks
Thomas R. Ortiz
Kelton E. Osborn
Steven M. Osborn
Mala Parikh
Thomas William Parks
Derek Thomas Payne**
Jennifer Pepe
Thomas Piekenbrock
Dorothy J. Pierson
Angela Pigg
Jean L. Pike
Todd Pilgreen
Patricia J. Pollock
Hadrian Predock
Jason Predock
Denise E. Purley
A. Christopher Purvis
Daniel G. Puzak
Rebecca L. Quigley
Larry Railey
Ruben Miguel Ramirez
Theodore C. Razatos
David Reddy
Peter R. Rehn
Ginny Reid
Rebecca J. Riden
Richard E. Rivera
Keith D. Robertson
Dennis Rodriguez
Timothy J. Rohleder

Christopher Romero
Rob P. Romero
Rachel Leah Rosenthal
Margaret Ross
Sunil S. Sakhalkar
Kenneth Sandoval
Alcides Santiesteban
Curtis J. Scharfenaker
James See
Lisa G. Sharp
Melanie L. Shelor
Curtis J. Simmons
Kimberly J. Smith
Richard V. Smith
David M. Somoza
Kira A. Sowanick*
Kevin D. Spence
Catherine Spencer
Joanne Spencer
Glade Sperry, Jr.**
Christopher M. Stachecki
Samuel M. Sterling*
Douglas W. Strech
John Scott Taylor
Kristen Taylor-Foley
Ross-Alan B. Tisdale
John C. Toomey
Hajime J. Uesato
Donald H. Vanderpool
Stephanie A. Vencil
James W. Visscher
Deborah Waldrip
E. Suzanne Weisman
Michael E. Wewerka
James I. Williams II
Elizabeth J. Wilson
Ronald A. Wilson
Jeffrey Winter
David Witherspoon
Kramer E. Woodard
John Woynicki
Jeffrey S. Wren
Jasmine C. Wu
Zeina A. Yazbeck
Alexia A. Zerbinis

* Associate
** Former Associate